It hit me one day
out of the blue
   that a truth
   that I knew
Was a little bit backwards—
That a little while back there
   we converged on an idea
that could use some re-thinking.
I think we
celebrate birthdays
   a little bit off.

We bake or buy cakes
and make a big show
To let birthday girls
and boys
know
That we love them

And I love that

Because it would do us all good
to feel special sometimes—
    at least once in a year,
And it's clear
    that a collection
    of well wishes
is well worth it.

So this is not a protest.

But if I focus
    my energy
In the first place
On that first day
and change birthday
To birth day

I'll find you.

And for all those birthday cakes
with one more candle,
For every year you had to handle
    my mess
And let me be the center
    of attention,
You never mentioned
the real hero...

Was you.

Every year on "my" birthday
I get presents
even though the day we remember
Came through your painful labor,
When you gave me life
And present-ed me to the world.

All I did was come out
    and scream.
I'm sorry to say that wasn't the
    last time that happened
And maybe wasn't even
    the most painful.

What I'm saying
is that maybe
I realize
On my birthday—
    that I should be the one
    giving you presents.

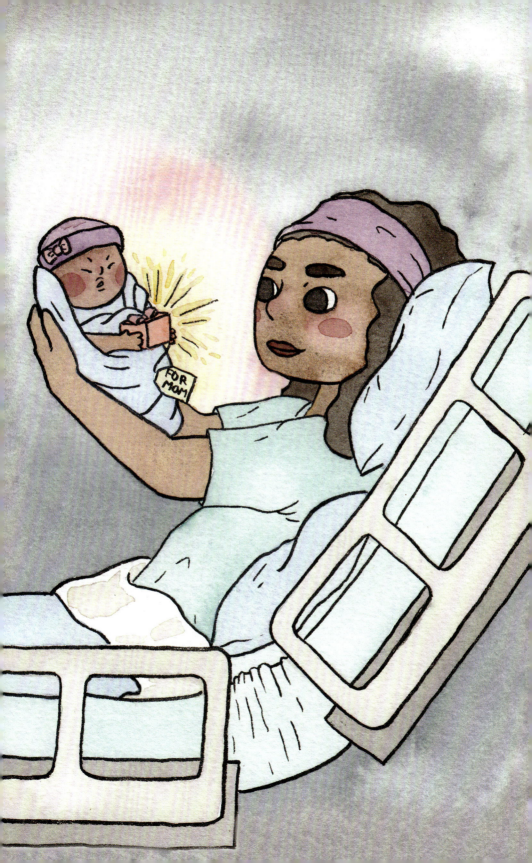

I mean, I took up room
   in your womb
Until you had to expand
And to have me
You had to put a hold
   on your plans.

And I never stopped to ask
If you could get back to them,

But I did stop to ask
if you could get me a
happy meal.

A lot.

And I didn't understand
Why you wouldn't give me
all that I wanted.

But I do now.

I wanted to stay home from school
    and stay up late at night
I wanted to watch violent movies
I always put up a fight

I wanted candy
And soda
And toys—
You said NO

I wanted to skip out on helping
And family—
You said GO

If I wanted the easy way out—
Not a chance.
I know now
that you always
    just had
Bigger plans.

And I'm glad now
that all of those NOs
Turned to knowing.

Like knowing
   that it's nice
   to be nice
And the price
   of doing right
   can be high,

But it's worth it.

Or knowing that
if I got all I wanted,
I'd be spoiled—
I'm sorry, again,
for all of your plans
that I foiled.

And I'm sorry

I know it's not fair
I kept secrets
   from you.
But I assume now
you knew
A lot more
than I knew
Because I know now
you know
A lot more
than I know.

... Except maybe
When downloading
photos
on phones...

But I know it's ironic
I'd say,
"You don't understand"
And now I use you
like google
For all of my questions—

How do I get red stains out again?
What if the medicine is expired?
   Oh yeah, and is it over the counter?
What flower is this?
What if this thing has been cooking forever
   and it doesn't look done?
How much is a stamp?
Uhhh... so... do I need to clean that?

And while we're on
    the subject of sorries—
I'm sorry
I borrowed
    so much of your stuff
And didn't manage to bring
    so much of it back.
I'm sorry simple questions
    put me on the attack.

I'm sorry that
I thought my "friends"
were so important,
And that I made you
transport me
    without regard for
    your time.
I'm sorry I haven't spent
more of my life
learning all the lessons
You would have taught me
    for free,

That I didn't take your advice
when you said "go read a book,"
I'm sorry I never even tried
    to help cook
And made a fuss not to eat
all the food that you made
AKA the food that I'm still craving now
    every day.

I would even go back
for the veggies
    if I could.
Believe me I know
ramen isn't that good
    every night.

I'm sorry I didn't clean more
   to take a load off of you.
Or do some loads of laundry.
Or learn more of your skills.

I'm sorry I didn't recognize
how the bills
just
pile up
And how your life
got
tied up
By my life.

I'm sorry I didn't go with you to
grandma's more.

I can't count
the I TOLD YOU SOs
   that I know
You could gloat about
   now,
But I'm glad
you don't bring them up
...that much...

And to know
that you won't ever
Give up
on me.

We might not have the money
   to leave very fancy heirlooms,
But no ring
   or diamond necklace,
No expensive rugs in a front room
could get me to trade my history
Or what you have passed down to me
And I'm grateful for the fortune,
   that I get from you, my mother:

A laugh that I've grown into,
Patience,
Charity, and
Charm.
Caring about others
And protection against harm.

I hope I get the fortune
    of your wit,
Your persistence to get through
    the... mess
Your determination through your
    children's stress
And somehow turn it into
    the happiness
that I can see now
in your eyes
Even if it took me
so, so long
to recognize.

So thanks
for those nine months
And all those years,
Thanks and sorry for the tears.
My biggest fear
　　is that I can't express
　　just how I feel—
It's bigger than the earth
　　and sky
　　and clouds
But the closest thing language
allows is

I love you.

Hi Mom

Written by Miles Petty

Illustrations by Julia Peterson

Interior design and layout by Wyatt Petty

Available at: www.thecaretree.com